"In The Style Of..."

100**SLIDE**LICKS
FOR**BLUES**GUITAR

Master 100 Slide Guitar Licks in the Style of the World's 20 Greatest Blues Players

LEVI**CLAY**

FUNDAMENTAL**CHANGES**

100 Slide Licks For Blues Guitar

Master 100 Slide Guitar Licks in the Style of the World's 20 Greatest Blues Players

ISBN: 978-1-78933-151-6

Published by **www.fundamental-changes.com**

www.fundamental-changes.com

Over 11,000 fans on Facebook: **FundamentalChangesInGuitar**

Instagram: **FundamentalChanges**

For over 350 Free Guitar Lessons with Videos Check Out

www.fundamental-changes.com

Cover Image Copyright: Star Singer Slide. Used by permission.

A huge thanks to Dolfinn at **www.starsingerslides.com** for making some of the best sounding and coolest looking slides on the market! (check out that cover!)

Contents

Introduction

For over 100 years, adventurous guitar players around the world have taken to using various objects – metal pipes, bottle necks, even medicine bottles – as movable frets on their instruments.

Originating from the "slack-key guitar" style of Hawaii, and the African-imported slave music/blues of mainland USA, slide guitar has evolved dramatically over a century. So much so, that sometimes it's incredible to think that the branch you're on stemmed from the same tree as another slide player.

In part this is due to the relatively uncommon use of the slide among guitar players. That's not to say it's not practiced by many people, but compared to other guitar playing tools – like the capo or pedals – it surprises me how many guitarists I meet around the world who have never even held a slide, let alone practiced with one. The result is that guitarists who base their playing around the slide have a much easier job of creating a style unique to them, instead of following the same path as millions of others.

For those new to this style, I'd encourage you to get a grasp of the content in my two previous Fundamental Changes books, *Delta Blues Slide Guitar* and *Slide Guitar Soloing Techniques*. These books will teach you everything you need to know about what a slide is, how it works, and all the associated techniques.

This book is aimed at the intermediate player who wants to explore the style of various well-known slide guitar players, expand their musical horizons, and begin to develop their own musical vocabulary.

Those who have read my *100 Licks For Country Guitar* book will know that I'm a firm believer in the importance of *vocabulary*. Music is a language comprised of words, not letters. Knowing the blues scale but never having heard the blues would lead me to conclude you probably can't play the blues. Blues is a language made from well-established phrases and progressions. It's what makes the genre relatable. Of course, you should add your own twist to things, but if you don't tip your hat to tradition, you'll just sound out of place. I liken it to Allan Holdsworth playing on an Albert King record, or Chet Atkins sitting in with Zakk Wylde. Without taking anything away from these incredible players, they would be out of place simply because they speak different musical languages. Just knowing the alphabet won't get you by as an Englishman in El Salvador!

This book consists of 100 licks from 20 great slide players. The licks will give you an idea of what each player is about, but more importantly will arm you with some great vocabulary you can use in your playing. You won't just learn licks, however, you'll learn about the artists behind them, making you a master of both the style and the history.

Here are a few important things to consider before you continue.

Slide choice

There are numerous slides on the market, made from various materials. Where possible, I've tried to use something close to what the artist in question would have used. When the choice was left up to me, I opted for one of my Star Singer Slides (that beautiful, eye catching slide on the cover!). These are wonderful ceramic slides, hand made in Glastonbury, here in the UK. Each one has a unique crackle finish and they have the kind of weight I look for in a slide.

Tunings

The nature of slide guitar – using a straight bar to play the strings – lends itself to open tunings. While not all slide guitarists play in open tunings, the majority do. Different players, however, prefer different tunings, so pay attention to the description of each lick and make sure you're in the correct tuning before attempting it!

Setup and tone

This leads to the subject of setup and tone. Each of these artists sound very different (I'll give you tone pointers in each chapter), but one consistent theme that will help you play these licks easier and make them sound good is having a good setup on your guitar.

This isn't a book on setting up guitars, but here are a few pointers to help with slide playing.

Having a high enough action (vertical height of the strings from the frets), a straighter neck (achievable with truss rod adjustments) and maybe a slightly taller nut will all contribute to your ability to play slide well. If this is an area you're unfamiliar with, take your guitar to a professional and have them set it up for you.

I'd also recommend a string gauge that lends itself well to detuning. A set of 11-52s from Ernie Ball (the Burly Slinky set – they come in a red pack!) is a great place to start.

Finally, on the page that follows is the important "Get the Audio" information. A lot of effort went into recording every single lick for your study, so don't forget to spend time carefully listening to the audio, as well as studying the musical examples. One of the incredible things about slide guitar is that it doesn't lend itself well to the conventional western system of notation or tab. There's no effective way to illustrate the microtonal options slide provides, so listen to the recordings and do your absolute best to imitate them carefully!

Good luck!

Levi

Get the Audio

The audio files for this book are available to download for free from **www.fundamental-changes.com.** The link is in the top right-hand corner. Simply select this book title from the drop-down menu and follow the instructions to get the audio.

We recommend that you download the files directly to your computer, not to your tablet, and extract them there before adding them to your media library. You can then put them on your tablet, iPod or burn them to CD. On the download page there is a help PDF and we also provide technical support via the contact form.

For over 350 Free Guitar Lessons with Videos Check out:

www.fundamental-changes.com

Over 11,000 fans on Facebook: **FundamentalChangesInGuitar**

Tag us for a share on Instagram: **FundamentalChanges**

Chapter One – Duane Allman

Many would consider Duane Allman to be the perfect place to begin when learning slide guitar. He's a player who influenced a generation in the short 4-year period in which he was recording. Few people could have had such an incredible impact in such a short space of time, and this is testament to Duane's incredible musical vision.

Born in 1946 in Nashville, his family moved to Daytona Beach in 1957. Duane picked up an interest in guitar in 1960 when his brother, Gregg, purchased a Teisco Silvertone from Sears. The guitar caused fights, and this was solved when Duane got his own Silvertone after wrecking his motorcycle (a tragic case of foreshadowing). Music really brought the two together and they played in numerous bands before making it big.

Interestingly, both brothers were left-handed, but learned to play right-handed – probably due to the scarcity of left-handed guitars in the '60s. Some would argue that having one's dominant hand in control of the slide could give you significant benefit when playing, but this isn't an argument I'd make – just try playing slide left handed!

Duane picked up slide in 1968, using a glass Coricidin pill bottle to imitate the slide playing of Jesse Ed Davis and Ry Cooder on the Taj Mahal cut of *Statesboro Blues*. Duane was a natural and his use of the slide would quickly become a defining part of his sound.

Outside of his own bands, Duane started to become popular on the session scene where he added a touch of rock to R&B and soul records, recording with names like Clarence Carter, Aretha Franklin and Wilson Pickett. It was his legendary cut on Pickett's cover of *Hey Jude* that brought him attention from record execs and peers alike, landing him a role next to Eric Clapton on the seminal Derek and the Dominos album, *Layla and Other Assorted Love Songs*.

The defining period of Duane's career was the formation of the Allman Brothers Band, alongside his brother Gregg on piano/vocals and Dickey Betts on second guitar. The group showed promise with their 1969 release, *The Allman Brothers Band*, which they followed up in 1970 with *Idlewild South*. While neither album was a commercial success, their live performances carried good word of mouth, and the collaboration between Duane and Eric Clapton was enough to see 1971's live album, *At Fillmore East*, chart in days. The album went on to reach number 13 on the Billboard charts, going gold that year, and eventually going on to achieve platinum status in 1992.

Despite having a career spanning half a century, Duane's tenure with the band was short lived. He was killed in a motorcycle crash in Macon, Georgia, in October 1971. While the band would continue and grow (featuring stints of over a decade with both Derek Trucks and Warren Haynes – two other slide masters found in this book), Duane's musical fingerprint served as the DNA for the band and influenced countless guitarist the world over.

When it comes to sound, Duane was well known for his stunning Gibson Les Pauls –both a '57 Goldtop, a '59 Standard Cherry Sunburst and, towards the end of his career, a Tobacco burst nicknamed "Hot Lanta" which he acquired from Billy Gibbons of ZZ Top. He was also known to play Stratocasters from time to time, and a '61 Gibson SG for some slide work (probably due to the incredible upper fret access provided by the design of the guitar).

Amp-wise, he was fond of a 1969 Marshall Super Bass – one of the iconic "plexi" models Marshall made during this period. While he owned a Dalla Arbiter Fuzz Face pedal, he would more often than not just run straight into the amp and play loud.

Duane was most well known for using open E tuning (E, B, E, G#, B, E), though there are examples of him playing slide in open A (E, A, E, A, C#, E), and standard tuning

Finally, there's the slide. He continued to use a medicine bottle, like the one he'd first picked up, and wore this on his ring finger. While these glass bottles are no longer produced, many companies offer replicas, such as the Planet Waves Glass Bottle Slide.

Now, onto the licks!

When it comes to playing slide, Duane takes full advantage of the barred position that open E tuning provides and bases a good 80% of his playing around this.

When playing rock in E, combining the notes on the 12th fret with those on the 10th fret gives you enough potential vocabulary to learn hundreds of classic licks. See the diagram below.

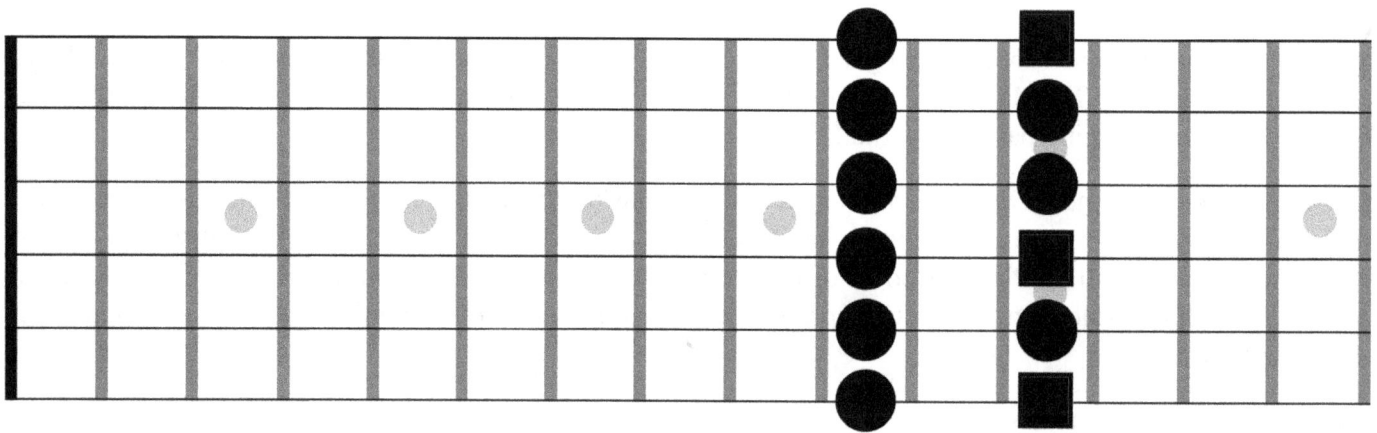

As an example, here's a lick similar to something Duane played on *Trouble No More*.

Beginning with a slide up to the root note (E) on the 12th fret, notice that all the notes are located on the 10th, or 12th fret. Think of the 12th fret as "home" and the 10th fret as notes for melodic embellishment you can use before going home.

Listen carefully to the audio for this lick as standard notation can't capture details such as how slow a slide is from one note to another. I've tried to include as much detail as possible (like the 11th fret bluesy notes that slide up into the 12th), but nothing will be quite like the recording.

Example 1a

The second example continues with this idea, but now higher up the neck as the underlying chord is a D. Home is now all the way up at the 22nd fret!

After playing a simple melody for two bars, I come down to that same root note (D) on the second string, 15th fret, and play a similar idea to the first two bars, but now an octave lower.

This lick should remind you of Duane's stellar playing alongside Eric Clapton on the Derek and the Dominos classic, *Layla*.

Example 1b

The next lick might remind you of *Statesboro Blues*. This example really milks the bluesy b3 (F) on the 9th fret of the third string. In the notation I've written *bends* rather than *slides* to indicate that the notes are slowly pushed up, as opposed to quickly slid.

The second part of the lick shift up three frets higher than the "home" position on the second and third strings. This highlights the 5th (A) and b7th (C) of the underlying D chord – which is perfect when you want to emphasise the D Minor Pentatonic (D, F, G, A, C) sound that's so prominent in rock music.

Example 1c

The final two examples move away from the overplayed minor sound and are based on chord progressions in E Major.

The first of these alternates between E Major and A Major – chords I and IV in the key of E Major – so the notes of the E Major scale (E, F#, G#, A, B, C#, D#) are going to work well here.

Example 1d begins with a slide into the home position at the 12th fret and continues with a repeating triplet. Care needs to be taken over the sudden shift up to the 17th fret to play a simple melody in the second bar.

The second half of the lick is played over the A Major chord. While the notes of E major are still in use, because the chord is A Major, the new home position is at the 17th fret.

Example 1d

The final example takes inspiration from the Allman Brothers classic, *Melissa*. The chords move between E Major, F#m11 and E/G#. This can be seen as a simple I to ii progression in E Major, with G# added to the bass to keep some interesting movement.

The notes used here are largely found in an E Major triad (E, G#, B) but with the addition of slides from below and a killer slide up to the 17th fret towards the end.

11

Example 1e

As you can see from just the short examples in this chapter, Duane's style is instantly accessible to almost any slide player, no matter how new the technique is. Listen to his music and be inspired by how willing he is to just experiment and look for melodies. He's not the most advanced player, but there's a reason he's one of the most influential.

Chapter Two – Ry Cooder

Although he's not one of the household names in this book, there can be little argument that Ry Cooder is one of the players most widely heard and respected by his peers.

Born in LA in 1947, Cooder is one of those artists who claims to have started playing guitar at such a young age that it's hard to believe, first picking up the instrument at just three years old! By the age of eight, he was reasonably adept on his instrument and decided to take things seriously.

While still in high school, he got the opportunity to play banjo with bluegrass legends Bill Monroe and Doc Watson in a thrown-together outfit, when Monroe's proper band found themselves stranded after a bus breakdown. While this didn't turn into a dream gig touring the country, it was a sign that music could be a serious option for Cooder.

At 17, Cooder was part of the original lineup for the band Rising Sons. While they didn't achieve success, the group became well known when Cooder and singer Taj Mahal found cult followings in later years.

After Rising Sons, Cooder went on to join Captain Beefheart and his Magic Band, recording guitar on 1967's *Safe as Milk*. But despite the promise this project had, the eccentricities of singer Don Van Vliet didn't gel with Cooder's musical ethos and he left suddenly in the same month the album came out.

From here Cooder turned his hand to session work and releasing his own music. To say his session career was a success would be an understatement. With over a thousand credits as guitarist on AllMusic, it's fair to say Cooder was a go-to name for anyone requiring authentic slide guitar.

As a session player Ry worked with The Rolling Stones, Van Morrison, The Monkees, The Beach Boys, The Everly Brothers, The Doobie Brothers, James Taylor, Eric Clapton and many more.

Outside of his session playing, his work as a composer for his own albums and film soundtracks is equally impressive and extensive. He has produced 17 solo albums spanning nearly 50 years and 17 film soundtracks (including the iconic guitar romp, *Crossroads*). If you're looking for a place to start, nowhere makes more sense than 1970's *The Slide Area*.

As a player, Ry hops genres like most guitarists hop notes. You'll find everything from authentic blues to folk, Gospel, pop, Tex-Mex, calypso, Hawaiian and Cuban sounds on his records. He's extremely hard to pin down to one style, which makes presenting just five licks in his style tricky! In fact, if you manage to get some of his slide licks down, you could still spend a lifetime working on his fluid fingerstyle approach to rhythm.

When it comes to gear, Ry has used a lot over the years, but he's best known for his two Strats. The first is a '67 Daphne Blue, which has undergone many mods, eventually settling on a Guytone pickup in the neck and a custom-built steel guitar pickup in the bridge. His main guitar is his iconic "Coodercaster", built from a Buddy Holly replacement body and a custom-made neck. This was eventually fitted with a Valco steel guitar pickup in the bridge (with base plate) and a cheap Teisco pickup in the neck.

Ry plays in several tunings, but most commonly open G (D, G, D, G, B, D) for rhythm guitar, and open D (D, A, D, F#, A, D) for lead. He often uses flatwound strings (10–50) on the blue Strat, and D'Addario Jazz Light 12-52 strings on the Coodercaster.

As a session player who lived through the '80s, Ry's amp choice varied greatly depending on the era. He has used everything from a custom-made Dumble amp, to rack systems that would rival the Starship Enterprise. The same is true of effects: if it existed, there's a chance Ry tried it!

In terms of slides, Ry is most commonly seen with a glass bottleneck-style slide, which he wears on his pinky finger.

Now, onto the licks!

Before looking at some lead guitar work, it makes sense to examine Ry's incredible rhythm work. Much like Eddie Van Halen, who is thought of as one of the all-time great rock soloists, Ry is best known for his unrivalled slide playing. In reality, however, his right hand work is just as impressive and considerably more subtle. Just one of Ry's albums will provide enough for a lifetime of learning before you even pick up the slide. Check out the rhythm guitar on a song like *On a Monday* or the intro to *The Very Thing That Makes You Rich (Makes Me Poor)*.

Example 2a is played in open G tuning and arranged so that the notes ring out to hold that G Major chord sound in the ear.

Wearing the slide on the pinky finger makes fretting the first chord easy. This is followed by a pull-off to the open strings, then a slide up to the 5th fret on the first string.

Note that the hammer-on to the 2nd fret, fourth string, can be played with either the slide or a finger. Other than that, you're using the slide for all single-note runs.

Example 2a

The next example explores the possibilities of open G further by introducing the low string, using the slide to play barred chords at the 3rd, 5th and 12th frets.

You'll notice that the final bar contains the same ending as the last idea. Clichés become clichés for a reason – they sound great, so you keep using them!

Example 2b

When it comes to Ry's lead work, you're looking at the very pinnacle of what slide guitar is about. It's the sound you hear in your head when someone says, "Slide guitar…"

Here's a lick played on an up-tempo blues in Bb. I've kept this in open G and played around the 3rd fret, though Ry may play something like this by placing a capo on the 3rd fret, allowing him to use open strings.

The important detail here is how you slide between the notes. You'll need to check out the audio, but as a guide, if I'm sliding from the 3rd to 4th fret, I don't just slide up – I drop down a bit *before* sliding up. This is impossible to notate, but it's key to getting Ry's sound.

Example 2c

Here's a lick that's a little slower and gives you the chance to really milk the slides between notes. It's similar to what Ry might play on something like *Dark End of the Street*.

This idea sticks strictly to the G Major Pentatonic scale (G, A, B, D, E) and comes to rest around the home position barre at the 12th fret.

As with the last lick, when sliding between multiple notes, dropping down a bit before sliding up to the next note really adds some expression to the lick.

Example 2d

The final lick exploits this single-string sliding concept by covering an entire octave using the G Minor Pentatonic scale (G, Bb, C, D, F).

Begin at the 8th fret and be careful with the intonation when sliding up the scale (and dropping down a bit before sliding up!)

Example 2e

Ideas like this can (and should) be fully exploited. Try different scales, ascending and descending. Play them quietly; play them loud. It's all about developing accuracy of intonation, control and vibrato. Slide guitar is one of the most expressive ways to play music, so explore every nuance as much as possible.

I can't stress this enough: Ry's playing is so broad and unique, it's impossible to cover him in just five licks. It would be easy to fill a whole book on his style and even then we'd only be scratching the surface. Go and listen to his music and catch the bug!

Chapter Three – Brett Garsed

Born in Victoria, Australia, in 1963, Brett Garsed is one of the obvious wildcards included in this book. After almost 40 years on the scene, Garsed is best known as one of the fathers of modern rock fusion and legato playing, more than a slide player. Yet he's a wonderful slide player with unique things he brings to the table. Garsed was the reason I personally decided to take up slide playing.

Brett picked up the guitar aged 12 after listening to Deep Purple, but it was hearing Ric Formosa playing on the Little River Band track *Every Day of My Life* two years later that encouraged him to buy a chrome slide to try to get that sound.

In Brett's own words, "The results were absolutely terrible, as I was in standard tuning and had no idea about anything like intonation, vibrato and muting."

This first attempt knocked Brett back until he saw a video clip of Joe Walsh playing *Rocky Mountain Way*. The footage was good enough to see exactly what Walsh was doing. On the advice of a friend, Brett picked up a cheap Les Paul copy, tuned it to open E and began to play more seriously.

After developing some control of the technique required to play with the slide, he went back to standard tuning and quickly realised that the tuning between the G and B strings made playing 3rd intervals quite difficult. As he wears the slide on his middle finger, he tried angling the slide and this did a great job. Suddenly he could access a lot of the classic open tuning ideas in standard tuning.

Other influences included Sonny Landreth's technique of fretting behind the slide and the playing of Rory Gallagher, but in his own words,

"When I play slide, the guy I hear in my head is David Lindley. I loved how he played beautiful, soaring slide in a 'non-blues' context with Jackson Browne. So as well as just showing me how it's done, he also made me realise that slide guitar could be used in any musical context. I now know that this is obvious, but for a kid living in an isolated part of Australia with no one around to ask for advice or guidance, this was a moment of self-realisation that would have a huge impact on how I would play slide, when I would play it and how I would make it work in a variety of musical situations."

As a recording artist, Brett's list of credits is extensive: from sideman work with John Farnham and Nelson, to seminal fusion recordings like *Centrifugal Funk* (with Frank Gambale and Shawn Lane). *Quid Pro Quo* (with 8-finger tapper TJ Helmerich), and his solo albums, with 2002's *Big Sky* being a masterpiece.

Regarding guitars, Brett is a long-time endorser of ESP guitars, who have released two signature models. Sticking mostly with standard tuning, he uses 11 gauge strings with a medium action, wearing his glass slide on the middle finger.

Let's explore some Garsed licks!

Wearing the slide on the middle finger is an integral part of this first lick, inspired by the stellar playing on his track *Drowning,* as you'll need the other three fingers for fretting notes. In order to achieve this, wear the slide down to the second knuckle, so you're still able to bend the finger.

Play the ascending scale with your fingers, then transition to playing with the slide for the final note in the second bar. This note is held and allows you to use expressive slide vibrato before going back to playing fretted notes.

As with most things slide, this really isn't designed to be notated, so pay attention to the text above the notation and listen to the audio!

Example 3a

An interesting aspect of Garsed's playing is how he exploits aspects of standard tuning to give the impression of a more common open tuning as the next example illustrates.

When barring on the D, G and B strings, the notes form a major triad with the 3rd on top. So, any time you're going to play the 3rd of a chord on the B string, you can rake into it with the notes on the D and G strings, because they're going to be in that chord too.

Notice the rake into the 12th fret in the first bar of Example 3b, implying a G Major triad, then a C Major triad in the final bar.

Example 3b

Example 3c covers a huge range of the guitar, from the 24th fret all the way down to the 4th. If you're playing a guitar that doesn't have that many frets, don't fret (sorry!) Actual frets aren't needed to make notes with the slide, so you can just slide up to where the 24th fret would be.

The main focus of this lick, and a unique feature of Brett's playing, occurs in the second bar. Towards the end you'll see I've put the note played at the 14th fret on the G string in brackets. This note isn't played with the slide. Instead, Brett would fret this with the pinky finger of his fretting hand – kind of like a backwards Sonny Landreth! It's very cool and a great way to work around the limitations of slide playing with standard tuning.

Example 3c

The next example takes the technique of fretting while playing slide even further, playing notes both in front of, and behind the slide.

Begin with the slide barred at the 9th fret, playing the D, G and B strings, then hammer on with the ring finger at the 10th fret before returning to the slide. The second bar sees you hammer from the 9th fret (played with the slide) to the 11th fret with the finger.

This sound has an undeniable pedal steel influence, so use your bridge pickup, a good clean tone, and some heavy compression to imitate this incredible instrument.

Example 3d

The final example showcases Brett's fluency in angling the slide to play double stops that are not located on the same fret. This technique is almost impossible to pull off with the slide on any finger other than the middle one, so don't kill yourself with frustration trying this with the slide on the pinky!

Begin by playing with the slide parallel at the 14th fret and, as you slide down, begin to angle the slide to allow you to play the 11th and 10th frets simultaneously.

A similar idea occurs in the next bar. Hold the slide at the 14th fret for the A Major triad, then slide up to the 18th and 17th frets to play two more notes in that A Major triad.

As with the previous example, this gives the impression of a pedal steel guitar. Obviously, this has its limitations, but if you need a low rent pedal steel sound, this will get you close enough.

Example 3e

Chapter Four – A.J. Ghent

A.J. Ghent is another odd choice for this book as he's not strictly a "slide guitarist". He does, however, give us an excellent opportunity to talk about lap and pedal steel guitarists and their influence on slide guitar. Not to mention that A.J. is an outrageously talented musician who continues to influence musicians of all backgrounds.

Ghent is definitely one of the younger names in this book, being born in Florida in 1986.

Considering the rich musical heritage in A.J.'s family (which includes steel guitar pioneers such as Willie Eason and Henry Nelson, who brought the "Sacred Steel" sound to the world) Ghent took an interest in the instrument at the relatively late age of 12.

After some time in Florida, Ghent relocated to Atlanta, Georgia, where he was taken under the wing of the legendary Colonel Bruce Hampton (best known for Aquarium Rescue Unit). This brought him immediate legitimacy as Hampton invited him to front his then band, Pharaoh's Kitchen. Being part of the jam band scene, Hampton's fans are avid archivers, so there are plenty of bootleg recordings to be found from this period.

As a solo artist, Ghent released *Live at Terminal West* in 2015 and his debut studio album, *The Neo Blues Project*, in 2018. Both have a somewhat cult following on the blues scene.

Despite being namechecked by top players like Jimmy Herring and Derek Trucks, it was a viral YouTube video (AJ Ghent and his Singing Guitar) that brought A.J. to the attention of the wider public. This short clip showcased a live solo filmed at his album release party. To this day I've yet to hear anything closer to the sound of the human voice played by a slide guitarist. Despite being able to see him playing, every time I watch it, I keep thinking a singer is in the background doing her best Beyoncé or Mariah Carey impression!

As mentioned above, A.J. actually plays a hybrid of slide guitar and lap steel, so it's worth talking about the lap and pedal steel tradition he comes from.

The lap steel guitar is played with the strings parallel to the ground and a metal bar that acts like a slide. There's no fretting of the strings. The instrument often has 8 or 10 strings and is tuned to an open tuning.

The pedal steel guitar is an answer to the limitation of these open tunings and takes advantage of the stationary nature of the instrument. It has a series of foot pedals and knee levers that allow the player to change the pitch of strings while playing. This enables you to create beautifully expressive parts without being limited by the open tuning you're using. Players like Buddy Emmons, Paul Franklin Jr, and Robert Randolph are shining examples of the instrument and I urge you to check them out immediately.

A.J.'s main guitar is a custom built 8-string that looks like a cross between a Telecaster, a Stratocaster, and a Les Paul, with a set of Lollar steel pickups thrown in for the authentic sound. He uses a tuning that is a hybrid of open D, with a B and E on top, but Ghent does mix this up depending on the song.

As for the slide, A.J. uses a heavy steel bar and plays with his hand over the top of the neck. This is interesting, but his technique can obviously be adapted to a more traditional slide guitar approach. For the sake of continuity, I've recorded these examples with a traditional slide on my ring finger.

Let's take a look at those licks!

The first example instantly gives you an idea of how hard these licks are to play on a standard slide guitar. In theory, this is a simple single-string lick in A Major, but getting it to sound like a human voice (or even just getting the intonation spot on for the faster 16th note runs) seems impossible!

There's no avoiding it: this will just take time.

Example 4a

Here's a shorter example, again on the high E string. This time the challenge comes with the addition of the chromatic passing note at the start of the 16th note run. The goal here is to achieve good definition between each note, rather than aimlessly sliding between pitches.

Example 4b

The next example expands on the theme of the last two licks but adds more complex rhythmic ideas.

One of the signs of a confident improviser is not needing to start on beat 1 of a bar, and in this case you begin on the second 1/8th note triplet of beat 2. This might take some time to get comfortable with, but it will give your licks a more laid-back feel.

Example 4c

Example 4d ramps up the difficulty with a long scalar run that spans most of the second bar. Aside from accuracy with the intonation, the other challenge here is keeping the note sustaining. This can be achieved with a compressor pedal, or some overdrive to help the notes sing a bit.

As with each example in this chapter, the notes are pretty basic, all coming from the A Major scale (A, B, C#, D, E, F#, G#). It's all about how well those notes are executed which brings the music to life.

Example 4d

For the final example, I've decided to look at some of A.J.'s rhythm work, inspired by a clip of him playing a standard 6-string guitar tuned to open E.

One of the benefits of playing with your hand over the top of the neck is that you can fret a chord like A Major at the 5th fret, but allow the B and high E strings to ring open, thus turning a garden variety A Major into Aadd9. Do the same when moving the chord up two frets to B Major, and the open strings create a Badd11.

Each note here is played with the slide, so you'll either need to have your slide over the top of the neck, or ensure it's not touching the first two strings to execute those chords.

Example 4e

Chapter Five – Billy Gibbons

Born in Texas in 1949, Billy was the son of musical parents (his father was a concert pianist and conductor) who bought him a Gibson Melody Maker for his 13th birthday.

Billy played in many bands in his youth but found success before he was 20 when he released his first record, *Flash*, with the group Moving Sidewalks.

Despite this group showing promise, Gibbons would cement his legacy by forming ZZ Top in Houston in 1969, where Billy, Dusty Hill and Frank Beard (ironically un-bearded!) have stayed for an incredible 50 years.

ZZ Top's First Album, released in 1970 was a solid blueprint for what would follow and you can instantly understand why the group has been so popular – from Billy's unmistakable vocal style to the rocking rhythm section and tasty blues rock soloing… There's even some pedal steel guitar on *(Somebody Else Been) Shakin' Your Tree*!

Billy's playing style is a blend of many influences, from the authentic blues he grew up on, like B.B. King and slide maestro Muddy Waters, to the sounds of '60s guitar icons such as Eric Clapton in Cream and Jimi Hendrix (Jimi and Billy actually became good friends).

Slide makes a debut on the group's 1972 album, *Rio Grande Mud*, on the track *Just Got Paid*. It's something Billy comes back to time and again on songs like *Tush* (from 1975's *Fandango!*), *Dust My Broom* (1979's *Deguello*), and *Sharp Dressed Man* (1983's *Eliminator*).

There's not much information available on Billy as a slide player. He's never been much of a teacher and if you ask him a question, his long-time tech Elwood Francis says you're likely to get a "colourful story". Aside from the obvious influences then, it's hard to say how Gibbons landed on his particular style. I can tell you that he has a signature slide produced by Dunlop, the Rev Willy Slide, which is made from porcelain with thick walls for superior sustain, and back in the day he used a medicine bottle style slide. Regardless of the material, his slide is worn on the middle finger.

To say Billy has a large collection of guitars is an understatement. But, with many hundreds of stage guitars in the ZZ Top warehouse, it really comes back to two guitars: his '59 Les Paul (Pearly Gates) and his "Billy-Bo" Gretsch Jupiter Thunderbird. These are strung with extremely light stings (7s!). It's hard to say which he prefers for slide. It would be reasonable to assume he's sticking to 7-gauge strings as he most often plays slide in standard tuning or open E.

When it comes to amps, Billy has the stadium power rock setup. There might be a huge rack, but it really comes down to a Marshall style amp with some delay, and some Hendrix style octave fuzz with EQ.

In 2015, Billy released his first solo album, *Perfectamundo*, which he followed in 2018 with *The Big Bad Blues* (with his slide making an appearance on *Standing Around Crying*). It shows that after almost 50 years since getting started, he's still full of music.

Let's take a look at some of his licks.

First up is a riff in the style of *Just Got Paid Today*. The key here is wearing the slide on the middle finger to allow you to play fretted notes with the other fingers. This is a big part of Billy's slide playing as he seeks to integrate the slide with his normal playing.

Beginning in open E, there is a driving rhythm on the open strings before a slide up to the 12th fret and down to the 10th. While sitting on this D Major chord, a light vibrato can be applied as you arpeggiate the chord.

This is followed by a classic rock riff, with all the notes fretted, and the slide is reintroduced for the final slide up to the 12th fret.

Example 5a

When it comes to soloing, Billy's style is incredibly simple. Instead of choosing to milk as much as he can from some simple, well-integrated ideas, he usually relies on going to areas of the neck where he can play all the notes under the slide.

Example 5b is also in open E tuning and relies on sliding repeatedly between the 17th and 12th frets. With the 12th fret as home, sliding to the 17th fret on the B and G strings highlights the 6th (C#) and root (E) of the underlying E Major chord, both of which sound great.

In the last bar I've indicated a slide down from the 12th fret on the 3rd string. This should be played really slow to give you a mean blues sound.

Example 5b

Another excellent example of sticking to barred positions is this slick little melodic idea that alternates between D Major and A Major, before resolving back to E Major.

An idea like this would be next to impossible in standard tuning, but exploiting the open tuning and using the slide often results in some really easy ways to make music.

Example 5c

By contrast, the following example, inspired by *Sharp Dressed Man*, milks the barred home position to the max, in the same way Duane Allman would have approached it.

The lick is played at the 8th fret over a C Major chord, but you can easily move it to work over other chords (at the 5th fret over A Major, or the 10th fret over D Major, etc).

Refer to the audio to get a feel for just how slow some of the slides are between notes. This is how to make this sound like the blues.

Example 5d

The final example shows how Billy might stray from the barred position when looking for a melody. In this case we are dealing with the turnaround of a 12-bar blues on a faster tune like *Tush*.

Although the chord progression is D Major – C Major – G Major, Billy might treat this as though it's all over a G chord and play the same basic two-fret pattern common to blues rock slide players. The addition here is the shift up three frets to the 18th position on the high E string for a bluesy bend. This note can always be added above your basic home barred position.

Example 5e

As you've seen, Billy's slide playing isn't advanced by any stretch of the imagination, but that's the beauty of slide guitar: you don't need a whole lot of tricks up your sleeve to create one hell of a sound!

Chapter Six – Warren Haynes

Born in North Carolina in 1960, Warren Haynes grew up on the sound of soul music and as a child sang along to the records of artists like Wilson Pickett and Otis Redding.

He picked up the guitar at the age of 12 and quickly became enamoured with the playing of Eric Clapton. As a singer, Warren was drawn to players who sang through their instruments: "When I listen to Bonnie Raitt or B.B. King, their voice is an extension of their instrument. All my life I have been looking for a guitar sound that is compatible with my voice."

After playing extensively in his home State, at the age of 20 Haynes landed a gig with Country music legend David Allen Coe. The gig lasted for 4 years and during this period Haynes rubbed shoulders with many industry pros and friends of Coe, one of whom was Dickey Betts, the surviving guitarist from the Allman Brothers (who had been in hiatus since 1982).

This friendship would result in Haynes joining Betts on his 1988 album, *Pattern Disruptive*, and becoming the obvious choice for guitar when Betts and Gregg Allman reformed the Allman Brothers in 1989 for their 20th anniversary. During this period the group released three studio albums: *Seven Turns* (1990), *Shades of Two Worlds* (1991) and *Where it All Begins* (1994), along with multiple live albums.

While this period of the group's history brought them to the attention of a new generation of music fans, relationships in the band were tense as both Betts and Allman spiralled out of control. This was exacerbated by an extensive touring schedule.

During this time Warren disbanded his Warren Haynes Band (with whom he'd released *Tales of Ordinary Madness* in 1993), and formed Gov't Mule with Allman Brothers band bassist Allen Woody. The Southern rock jam band found popularity with their self-titled 1995 album, which would lead to Warren opening Allman Brothers shows with Gov't Mule, then going on to play with the Allman Brothers later that night.

However, the internal friction in the band was enough to force Warren to leave the Allman Brothers, and he went out to make it with his new outfit.

While on his travels, Haynes got to play with Phil Lesh of the Grateful Dead (the iconic American jam band where Jerry Garcia made his name), and this eventually led to the reformation/evolution of the band under the moniker of The Dead, with Warren taking on guitar duties.

Warren re-joined the Allman Brothers after Betts left, this time alongside slide maestro Derek Trucks. Together they released just one studio album, 2003's *Hittin' the Note*, but as a band they would regularly perform right up to their final gig in 2014. When all is said and done, Warren played with the Allman Brothers for 22 years – as long as founding member Dickey Betts! So as far as having an influence on the group, Warren was very much a part of their DNA.

Warren owns a wide array of guitars, but much of his collection consists of Gibsons. While he can be seen with a Firebird, SG, or ES-335, Haynes is a Les Paul guy at heart and often plays his own signature model by Gibson, strung with 10-46 strings.

For amplification, he generally uses a Marshall style amp – usually a Diaz CD-100 and a Soldano SLO-100.

Warren favours a glass slide on his ring finger and uses a selection of tunings, but often opts for standard tunings, which he says, "…gave me more of my own voice. I could play stuff that was less conventional and less traditional."

Now, onto the licks!

First is a rock riff in standard tuning that uses the G Minor Pentatonic scale (G, Bb, C, D, F) with a combination of fretted notes and the slide. While this could easily be played with just the slide, Warren would use his fingers for more precise double stops, then the slide when he wants to add vibrato.

In the notation/TAB here, the notes with vibrato are played with the slide, while the rest are fretted. The key to nailing this lick is to make sure the slides into the notes are at the right speed for maximum effect.

Example 6a

In Warren's lead playing, you'll see a wonderful combination of traditional Allman-style slide influence and some of his own cool ideas.

The following example works over a typical rock jam in E Minor, using notes of the E Dorian mode (E, F#, G, A, B, C#, D) and can be seen as two separate ideas.

First is the open position lick part, sliding a picked note down a scale tone, then executing a pull-off to an open string. It takes a while to get the hang of pulling-off with the slide, but don't skip over this technique.

The second part of the applies pull-offs to an ascending line on the high E string. While this could obviously be fretted, using the slide allows you to subtly slide into the notes before the final slide up with vibrato.

Example 6b

Playing in standard tuning often means that some of those classic open tuning licks require a bit more work with the slide, as demonstrated in the next example.

This D Major pentatonic lick will give you an idea of how Warren deals with the limitations of standard tuning. The first measure translates pretty well, but the second measure (a classic Duane Allman style lick) is much trickier in this tuning. When you listen to Warren, his playing is rarely pitch perfect, but that's all part of the attitude.

The final part of the lick demonstrates Warren's willingness to fret notes when the slide presents too many problems. Fret the double stop-before sliding up to end the phrase higher on the neck.

Example 6c

Here's an idea Warren might play over some diatonic chord changes: F Major – C Major – G Major.

Despite all the chords belonging to the key of C Major, it's the G Major that feels like "home". But rather than picking one scale to fit over everything, here it makes sense to treat each chord as a new harmonic event. Analyse things a bit deeper and you'll see that over the F Major chord, the line slides into an A note (the 3rd of the chord). Over the C Major, there is a slide to an E (the 3rd of C Major), and over the G chord, a slide to a D (the 5th of G Major). Each time a chord lands, the note that is played happens to be in the chord and sounds good… there might be something to this!

Example 6d

The final example repeats the previous chord progression, but showcases the extreme range Warren likes to use when soloing, often going way beyond where his fretboard ends.

In bar 4, as the melody moves towards the F Major chord, it makes sense to land on an F note – the root of the chord. This moves down a semitone and leads nicely to E, the 3rd of C Major, followed by a slide way up to the 27th fret and a G note (the root of the G Major chord).

A nice aggressive vibrato is essential here. It will help to mask the pitch you're aiming for and make the listener's ear do some of the legwork.

Example 6e

Chapter Seven – Son House

Eddie James "Son" House Jr, was born in Mississippi in 1902, making him one of the undeniable fathers of the slide guitar tradition.

House led an interesting life and grew up in an time where there were still people who had lived through the era of slavery. Like many people with similar roots, religion became a big part of his identity. Verifiable records of his youth are hard to come by (as we'll see), but we do know that he worked as a preacher and had a disdain for secular music. He said, "I didn't like no guitar when I first heard it. Oh gee, I couldn't stand a guy playin' a guitar. I didn't like none of it."

Nevertheless, Son picked up the guitar around the age of 25 and, after making a little bit of money, he would focus his efforts into a career in music.

With music came drink, however, and in 1928 House shot a man dead at a party and was convicted of murder.

Somehow he managed to get out of his sentence after just a year, on condition that he left town. He relocated to Clarksdale and formed a friendship with fellow Delta blues guitar legend, Charley Patton. While the two shared a mutual love of music and booze, it's said that they were very different men and would argue often. Ultimately their respect for each other won through and Charley helped launch House's career when he joined him for a recording session for Paramount in 1930.

While these recordings weren't a huge success at the time, they were enough for respected ethnomusicologist Alan Lomax to seek House out in 1941 to record more for the Library of Congress.

The first thing you may notice here is more than a decade elapsed between these records. It's widely thought that House all but put the guitar down during this period. Some would say it was due to the constant internal struggle of being a man of God playing "the Devil's music". Others say it was a combination of missing fame and his friend Patton dying in 1934.

Such gaps weren't uncommon in House's history, and after making these recordings Son disappeared again, only to be found onve more by a group of blues enthusiasts and researchers in 1964! Having clocked up 20 years away from the guitar (Son seemed quite cheerful about this), the group eventually managed to persuade Son House to be Son House again.

He remained reasonably active in music from this time until Alzheimer's and Parkinson's disease forced him to hang up his guitar in 1976. He settled down in Detroit and passed away in the October of 1988, succumbing to cancer of the larynx.

When it comes to his sound, House's trademark was his National resonator guitar. Aside from this, it was just Son's fingers and a metal slide (worn on the middle finger) that did all the talking. He was known to play in both open G and open D tuning.

Son was a man who lived the blues. When he performed it, he wasn't playing a scale he read in a book, he was telling his story. There's nothing more authentic than that. Son House WAS the blues.

Let's take a look at some of his licks!

I want to preface these examples by saying that Son's playing is the hardest to emulate in this entire book. Not because of its technical challenges, but because his playing is so loose that it's easy to sound TOO clean when playing in his style. My advice is, just let it all ring out!

First up is a riff similar to that heard on his iconic *Death Letter Blues*.

Bend the note on the 3rd fret with your finger before switching to the slide for all other notes. When sliding into the 5th fret on the 1st string, let it ring out and play the 5th string against it to drive the rhythm on. This isn't exactly what House played, but the focus here is playing a note on the high string with a slide and letting the other strings ring out.

Example 7a

The next example is almost identical to the previous one, but attempts to capture some more of the flavour of House's playing.

Whereas in the previous example each note was picked with precision, here I'm strumming with my index and middle fingers, and putting an aggressive accent on the downstrokes.

When the slide note rings out, you can dig in and add some real noise underneath it to push the riff along.

Example 7b

Here's another slow blues riff, now in open D tuning.

The goal here is to really *hit* the guitar. Make noise. On its own this can sound a little odd, but in context – with Son's powerful voice bellowing over the top – it's quite a sound!

Example 7c

While Son's ideas are difficult to execute in the same he would have played them, it doesn't mean they are complicated, as demonstrated by the following lick.

This is similar to something Son might sing over. The idea simply requires you to repeatedly slide into the 12th fret and add a decent amount of vibrato. This doesn't need to be in tune, it just needs to be played with passion!

Example 7d

39

The final lick shows House's simple approach to outlining chord changes, this time in open G tuning.

In the key of G Major, we're moving from the IV chord (C), back to the I (G). In order to do this, Son would slide into the 5th fret area (home position for the IV chord), then down to the open position for a simple two note blues lick.

Example 7e

There's no denying the simplicity of Son's guitar playing, but if you spend some time listening to his recordings, you'll quickly understand how the power of his voice carried his career. As far as Delta blues guitarists go, there's not many better than Son House.

Chapter Eight – Elmore James

Elmore James (originally Elmore Brooks) was born in Mississippi in 1918.

James picked up music around the age of 12, playing the diddley bow (a single-string instrument consisting of a string stretched over a wooden board). By 14 he was out playing on the weekends and finding his sound by developing the ideas of those who influenced him, such as Robert Johnson and Tampa Red.

Despite playing regularly, James's recording career didn't begin until 1950, after the war (where James served in the Navy).

His first record was *Dust My Broom*, released in 1952, which was a surprise success. In large part this was due to the unique sound he'd crafted for himself, due to his work as a radio repairman. His skills allowed him to modify amplifiers to run at breaking point.

James bounced from record label to record label, recording 29 singles in total, but this was enough to land him the title of The King of Slide Guitar among music fans of the day. He was an influence on early Rock 'n' Roll music and the blues explosion of the '60s. One only needs to listen to a record like *The Sky Is Crying* to get a feel for just how ahead of his time he was.

Unfortunately, he wouldn't be around to see the extent of his huge influence, as he passed away of a heart attack in 1963 aged just 45.

There are very few pictures of Elmore, but we can see that he played a Silvertone 1361 and he appeared to wear a brass slide on his pinky finger. He often used open E and open D tunings.

James's slide influence is undeniabl. Many of the licks he pioneered became staples, played by everyone who picked up a slide after him.

Let's look at some of them!

It would be impossible to talk about Elmore James and ignore his most influential lick: the classic intro to *Dust My Broom*.

Begin by sliding into the 12th fret on the top 4 strings and apply a subtle vibrato as you continue to pick the chord. After you've created a strong sense of the underlying chord, it's time for a simple, single-note melody using the 12th fret home position and notes found two frets below. The licks aren't particularly refined, it's about sliding into that 12th fret knowing that it sounds good.

Example 8a

As one of the pioneers of single-note slide guitar soloing, James' licks are far from complicated. Most often he would stick to the basic home position and approach these notes from two frets below.

The following example would usually be played over the first four bars of a blues, though you could play this over the second four bars too.

The secret to making something like this your own is how you phrase it. Elmore slides so slowly between notes that using slides in the TAB felt wrong. Instead I opted for bends, but it's still all slide!

Example 8b

The next example is played over the last four bars of our blues in D Major and combines the same two-fret pattern from before with a great little turnaround/ending in the last two bars.

In bar 3, the descending chromatic note on the 5th string should be fretted. This will allow you to play the open 1st string against it before using the slide again to slide up to the 11th and 12th frets.

The lick finishes with a typical ending, but if you wanted this to be a turnaround, then instead of sliding to the 11th and 12th frets to play the root note, you can slide to the 6th/7th frets to play the V chord which pulls you back to the start of the blues progression.

Example 8c

Here's another blues intro in D using nothing more than the home position at the 12th fret and the notes found two frets below. Again, I've opted to use a combination of slides and bends in the notation, with the bends indicating a slow, bluesy slide.

Regarding the rhythms, I've notated this in 12/8 time and used some 4:3 tuplets. This is all very complicated and not something Elmore would have thought about – it's just a way of trying to explain what's happening. Nothing is set in stone here, just push and pull with the rhythm and express yourself.

Example 8d

Here's one final idea, this time showcasing one of Elmore's faster repeating licks leading to a blues turnaround. We're still sticking to the home position and adding notes two frets below.

In essence the idea is simple: play the 12th fret, move down to the 10th, then pick the 12th fret on the second string. While easy in theory, doing this with the slide introduces a lot of noise. However, this should be celebrated! It's the noise of transitioning between notes that make this a lick to play and not a great lick to notate!

Example 8e

Chapter Nine – Robert Johnson

Born in Mississippi in 1911, Robert Johnson is the pinnacle of the Delta blues and wrapped up in the mystery that surrounds the genre.

Despite being widely regarded as a legend, most of what we know of Johnson's life has been pieced together from document research and the people who claimed to have known him, or who knew people who knew him.

It's hard to say when Robert began playing, but we do know that he was hounded for playing secular music – the "Devil's music" as it was known. Robert would eventually let this idea grow, when it became rumoured that his astonishing guitar playing skills and gaunt appearance were a direct consequence of making a deal with the Devil (or perhaps the Haitian Vodou icon Papa Legba) at the crossroads.

From November 1936 to June 1937, Johnson is credited with 41 known recordings, featuring just 29 songs – and that was it. Just as suddenly as he appeared, he was gone. He died of unknown causes in August 1938 at the age of just 27. Nothing was reported at the time and we only know this to be the case because three decades later a musicologist researching Johnson's life discovered his death certificate.

Although his musical output was small, his influence is undeniable, and every great blues guitar player that followed would namecheck the man.

Robert's playing was as steeped in mystery as the man himself. We can't say for certain what guitar he played (though it's widely assumed to be the Gibson L-1 he held in one of only two confirmed authentic pictures of him). It's also impossible to say for certain what type of slide he used or which finger he wore it on. If you want that information, you'll need to go down to the crossroads…

Let's take a look at some of those trademark licks!

First up is a *Crossroads* style turnaround which I've written in open A tuning (though I believe Robert played the original in open A with a capo on the second fret, making everything sound a tone higher).

Begin with a slide into the 12th fret on the top strings, before sliding down to the open position for the classic two note Delta blues lick.

The second half of the lick is a classic Robert Johnson turnaround idea. Fret the notes in bar 3 with the index finger, then shift back to the slide in the final bar.

Example 9a

The thing that fascinates me most when listening to *Crossroads* is something Johnson does in the final two bars – playing a simple slide melody against a steady palm-muted note in the bass. This example explores that idea in a way that will facilitate looping.

First get used to playing a palm-muted open 5th string with your thumb to a metronome. Next, work on adding the melody against that pulse. It will come as no surprise that the melody notes all come from the home position at the 12th fret.

Example 9b

Example 9c explores this idea further, now with a melody that lasts for 2 bars.

As with the previous examples, I've recorded this in open A tuning. If you want to add a capo at the 2nd fret, that will bring you closer to Robert's sound.

Example 9c

The next lick continues with this idea. It's a turnaround in the style of *Come On In My Kitchen* in open G tuning.

Instead of playing the open 5th string on each beat, this time it's added underneath each of the high melody notes.

Begin by sliding into the 12th fret while playing the open bass note. Then slide down to the open position for a bluesy double-stop idea. This turnaround features the same descending chromatic note, but it's ringing out against the open high string.

Example 9d

The final example draws influence from *Ramblin' On My Mind*, and showcases Robert's love of combining slide melodies at the 12th fret with open position fretted riffs.

Apply a palm mute to all the notes in the open position and use the fretting hand index finger to play the notes at the 2nd fret. Apart from that, each note should be played with the slide.

Example 9e

As with each of the true Delta players in this book, it's impossible to nail their styles in just five licks, so do check out my book *Delta Blues Slide Guitar* to dig deeper into this fascinating style.

Chapter Ten – Sonny Landreth

Clyde "Sonny" Landreth was born in 1951 in Mississippi. After spending a few years in Jackson, his family relocated to Lafayette, Louisiana.

Taking his early influences from Scotty Moore and Chet Atkins, Sonny would go on to pioneer modern slide guitar playing, pushing the boundaries of technique as he developed his highly influential style.

Sonny got his start in the mid-to-late 70s as a session player, playing guitar and dobro for many artists including Tommy Bolin, Freddy Fender, Zachary Richard and Marti Jones.

Working in the Louisiana music scene brought a strong *zydeco* influence (a Cajun/Creole jazz blues fusion) to his playing, which can be heard on his 1981 debut, *Blues Attack*.

Landreth would go on to release 16 more albums, with notable efforts including 2008's *From the Reach*, and 2012's *Elemental Journey*.

As a slide player, Sonny is best known for his extensive use of fretting behind the slide to overcome the limitations of open tunings. His playing is that of someone with immense creativity and with the skill to express it to the listener.

Landreth's influence is far reaching and fans include Mark Knopfler, Warren Haynes, Johnny Winter and Eric Clapton. Each has worked with Sonny on record, with Clapton featuring him on multiple Crossroads Guitar Festivals.

For gear, Landreth is a big fan of the Stratocaster and Dumble amps. He uses multiple tunings on his records, but we can say for sure that he's a fan of the Dunlop 215 heavy glass slide, which he wears on his pinky finger.

Let's look at some Landreth-style licks.

First up is an example using Sonny's "Melodic tuning" – an interesting hybrid consisting of the notes E, A, E, A, B and C#. This one is a lot of fun, as the top three strings are tuned to the first three notes of the A Major scale, making melodies very easy to play.

In this example you'll need to lift the fingers behind the slide up, then use the picking hand to pluck the notes between the slide and the nut. This results in a unique, ethereal sound as you add the sympathetic resonance on the other side of the slide. Listen to the recording and you'll see what I mean.

Example 10a

Now we're going to apply a simple Travis picking pattern to this tuning to show just how easy it is to add a great melody to a picked bass pattern.

Use the thumb to alternate between the 5th and 4th string with a palm mute. Pick out the melody over the top, letting it ring, and apply a light vibrato.

The magic of this tuning is that playing the middle 4 strings gives you a sus2 chord. Adding the top string brings the 3rd into play and gives you an add9 chord.

Example 10b

Next up is a slick little solo idea in open G tuning that showcases Sonny's fretting behind the slide style.

Begin by sliding into the 12th fret on the top string. To play the note on the 10th fret, keep the slide positioned at the 12th fret and use the index finger to press the string down behind the slide. Each time you see a note in brackets in the TAB, that's requires fretting behind the slide.

Example 10c

Example 10d takes this idea even further and applies the concept to whole chords!

This is almost impossible to pull off with the slide on any finger other than the pinky, so give it a go. Pay careful attention to the TAB and fret everything in brackets behind the slide. This should be relatively obvious as (thankfully!) the slide stays at the 12th fret.

Add some light vibrato to taste and prepare to wow your friends.

Example 10d

Our final lick showcases just how awesome fretting behind the slide can be when you want to add a burst of speed to a solo.

Begin by tuning to open G Minor (D, G, D, G, Bb, D).

The trick here is to pull off from the note behind the slide before returning to the slide – that's right, a pull-off! Although the pitch is going up, in order to execute this cleanly you need to really pull off from the fretted 10th fret note, rather than just lifting your finger.

Aside from this technical aspect, the lick is relatively simple… it's just very fast! Take your time with it and get to grips with the fingering slowly, then build up speed over time.

Example 10e

Chapter Eleven – Joey Landreth

Another of the young, promising stars of slide guitar, Joey Landreth (amazingly no relation to Sonny Landreth!) was both in 1987, in Winnipeg, Canada.

Another child prodigy, Joey picked up the guitar aged around 7, when his father salvaged a Maya Telecaster.

Joey worked hard and found himself a niche as a desirable session musician due to his unique sound on the guitar, but fame came when he formed The Bros Landreth with his brother David. The group released *Let it Lie* in 2013 and picked up an American distribution deal in 2014. This would result in heavy touring around the US and Canada, finding an audience anywhere they went.

While this was happening, Joey continued to write and would release his own EP, *Whiskey* in 2017, and follow it up with his debut album, *Hindsight*, in 2019.

Although he's not been around for long, Joey exists in a time where access to music is easy. It's easy to find incredible live-in-the-studio videos and gear demos with a quick search on YouTube. Look up Joey Landreth and you'll find it's absolutely worth your time, as he's one of the most incredible musicians walking the earth. I appreciate that sounds like hyperbole, but give him a chance…

Joey mostly plays guitar in an open C tuning, though not the common C, G, C, G, C, E. Instead, he takes open D as his starting point and moves it down a tone, resulting in C, G, C, E, G, C – a trick he picked up from fellow guitar player Champagne James Robertson.

His choice to play in an open tuning at all times means he's had to learn how to get by playing covers, no matter what the chords. As such, he's developed an incredible ability to play harmony in the tuning, and not be slowed down by the slide. He's fluent in playing over changes and makes extensive use of fretting behind the slide to make this work when not playing a major chord. For strings, he's using 19, 22, 26, 42, 52 and 65 with a regular high action. He wears his signature Rock Slide brass slide on his pinky finger.

Let's look at his incredible playing!

First up is a typical rhythm guitar example Joey might play. It showcases how fluently he frets while playing slide, and also his impressive chord vocabulary (the open major tuning doesn't get in the way of any chord sound!)

The lick begins with some resonant vibrato at the 12th fret. Just place your slide there and apply vibrato without picking. The chord will sound, but very quietly.

The next two bars require you to play with the slide at the 12th fret, while fretting behind the slide at the 9th and 10th frets. Again, I've used brackets around these notes to help indicate the use of a fretting hand finger.

After sliding into an F chord, three bars are played without the slide. Here you'll find a great minor triad voicing for this tuning, along with a beautiful open string melody which you can really let ring.

Finally, when you get back to the low open string, it's back to the slide for a typical open position blues lick.

Example 11a

Next up is a lick that really focuses on fretting behind the slide. As with the previous example, any notes in brackets are fretted with a finger behind the slide and everything else is played with the slide.

There's a lot going on here, both technically and harmonically. Joey doesn't treat his tuning as a limitation and has a firm grasp of the harmony needed to get by in pop, rock, even jazz. This licks sounds like something between Bach and Charlie Parker... but with a slide! Take your time with it and focus on accurate intonation.

Example 11b

Now you've developed some basic proficiency in fretting behind the slide, here's a lick that takes you from the IV chord (F Major) back to the I chord (C Major) via the iv minor (F minor). Playing these minor triads with the slide alone is impossible, but removing the option from your vocabulary altogether would be a shame.

Bar one sits on an F chord at the 5th fret and features a percussive slap on beats 2 and 4 (indicated in the notation with the * symbol). Next, move up the neck playing the three F minor chord inversions shown, playing the notes in brackets with a fretting hand finger behind the slide. Apply a light vibrato to these chords to imitate a pedal steel guitar.

Example 11c

Now we have a beautiful jazzy/Gospel chord progression that takes the fretting behind the slide concept to the extreme.

The most important part of the technique of playing behind the slide is understanding that the slide itself must be kept straight in its position. For most chords it's obvious where the slide should sit, but with the F7/A chord it's easy to miss the fact that the slide sits at the 12th fret.

The best part of this idea is the slick movement from the Bb in bar 3, moving though chords back to the Bb. In the bass notes here there's a great descending movement of Bb (over the Bb chord), Ab (over Bb7), G (Eb/G), then Gb (Ebm/Gb). This descending chromatic movement using inversions is beautiful and something you'll absolutely never see from an average slide player.

Example 11d

Finally, we move away from fretting behind the slide to look at a lead idea played completely with the slide.

The interesting technique here is the sliding artificial harmonic at the end of the second bar. Place the slide over the 5th fret as normal, but place the index finger of the picking hand on the string over the 17th fret. With the picking finger in place, pluck the string with either the thumb or ring finger. This will create an artificial harmonic an octave higher than the slide. From here, use the slide to shift this note up an octave by sliding up to the 17th fret. This will result in an outrageously high-pitched note that's guaranteed to grab attention.

Example 11e

We're only scratching the surface here of what Joey is capable of. I hold him in the highest regard and think he's one of the most talented guitarists alive today. There's a treasure trove of things you can learn from him, so get to work!

Chapter Twelve – Bonnie Raitt

Born in California in 1949, Bonnie Raitt went on to become the first lady of slide guitar with a career spanning almost five decades and counting.

Raised in a musical family (her father was a Broadway music star and her mother a pianist), Raitt picked up guitar aged 8 and progressed quickly, taking an interest in slide playing early on.

As a singer/songwriter, Raitt's influences weren't just guitar players. Instead she took inspiration from the folk scene of the day, and artists such as Pete Seeger, Joan Baez, Woody Guthrie, Bob Dylan and Janis Joplin to name a few. This was combined with a love of the traditional blues slide players. She even opened gigs for Muddy Waters and John Lee Hooker in her early days.

Despite trying to avoid a career in music, Bonnie was eventually snapped up by Warner and handed a record deal. She released her self-titled debut album in 1971, and followed this up with 1972's *Giving it Up*, 1973's *Takin' My Time*, 1974's *Streetlights*, and 1975's *Home Plate*. Each of these albums was received well critically, but none were the big commercial success a label really looks for.

This all changed with the release of 1977's *Sweet Forgiveness*. Suddenly the dynamic in the record industry changed and big money was being thrown around to secure the next big act. With big money behind her she could take things to the next level, but as that happened, the positive critical reception died down. It seemed that success just wasn't meant to be.

In fact, it took more than 10 years before the magic happened. 1989's *Nick of Time* (her 10th album) achieved the critical and commercial success everyone knew she was capable of. This album secured Raitt a Grammy, went to number one on the US charts, and all these years later still makes it onto Rolling Stone's 500 Greatest Albums of All Time list.

She would go on to record 7 more albums, with the most recent (at the time of writing) being 2016's *Dig in Deep*. At the age of 69, she continues to write, record, and inspire generations of young musicians to see what's possible when you keep working and never give up.

Gear wise, Bonnie is a big user of the Stratocaster (being the first female to receive a signature model back in 1996). Her main axe is a combination of a '65 body and an unknown neck which she picked up for just $120 back in 1969. She's used that guitar on every gig since.

She uses a glass bottleneck style slide on her middle finger, and while she's used many tunings, the most notable is open A tuning (E, A, E, A, C#, E) – open G tuning shifted up a tone.

Let's take a look at some of her licks!

Example 12a is an open position lick that sits somewhere between A Major and A minor. With any new tuning, a great starting point is to get to grips with the bluesy minor pentatonic sound in the open position.

Example 12a

Next up we have some more melodic vocabulary around the home position at the 12th fret. As expected, Raitt draws a lot of her vocabulary from the home position and the notes two frets below.

The real treat here is the inclusion of the D note in bar 3. This nice passing tone takes us from major pentatonic to something more akin to the A Major scale.

Example 12b

Example 12c takes the previous idea and explores it a little further with another lick in A Major.

Begin at the 17th fret and move down to the home position at the 12th fret. Everything else is a mixture of the home position and notes two frets below.

Example 12c

The next example begins on the root note on the 5th fret of the high string, then moves up the A Major scale before it resolves to the home position at the 12th fret.

Bonnie has a wonderful vocabulary of major scale licks that are perfect for pop songs that have shifted away from a straight-up blues vibe.

Example 12d

The final example shows how Bonnie might play around a chord other than the A Major she's tuned to. In this case it's a melodic idea around an E Major chord. The solution is relatively simple – treating the 7th fret position as home and adding basic scalar ideas around this area.

Example 12e

Chapter Thirteen – Chris Rea

Born in Middlesbrough, England, in 1951, Chris Rea is the only guitarist featured in this book from my side of the pond. To his credit, it's a position well deserved – his impact as a composer and a slide player has influenced a generation of young English guitar players.

Impressively, Rea didn't pick up the guitar until his early 20s, when he found a deal on a 1961 Hofner V3 for just £32! Upon hearing Charley Patton, Chris sought out more experienced guitarists in his area to explain how Patton was getting the sound from the guitar. The answer was, of course, "a slide", so in Chris's own words, "That was it for me. I was gone from that day on."

Rea worked with a selection of bands in his early years, even recording guitar on Hank Marvin's 1977 release, *Hank Marvin Guitar Syndicate*. His debut album, 1978's *Whatever Happened to Benny Santini?* didn't see much success in the UK, but *Fool (If You Think It's Over)* would be Rea's biggest success in the US, reaching #12 on the Billboard Hot 100. The downside was that it didn't feature Chris playing any guitar!

His next few albums were anything but hits and Chris would often argue that this was due to the record label trying to smooth out his harder blues side for more commercial appeal. Eventually, Rea realised this wasn't going to work and in 1983 he released *Water Sign*. This album wasn't an immediate success, but with strong touring support across the UK and Europe, the album suddenly caught on and sold half a million copies.

His next record, 1985's *Shamrock Diaries* was the start of major success and from here, each successive album sold extremely well. Ultimately, while Chris was never considered "cool" with the youth, he managed to find a solid market. While that market might have been dads driving in their cars, the fact was they were reliably buying records. Chris had made it.

When it comes to guitars, Chris is a Strat man (having his own signature model at one point). His main axe is a '62 Candy Apple Red (affectionately known as "Pinkey") that he has played since the beginning of his career. He uses a pair of Fender Blues Juniors on stage with drive coming from a tube screamer, a compressor, and occasionally a delay or chorus pedal.

His main tuning is open E and he plays with a glass slide on his pinky finger.

Let's look at some of Chris's licks.

First up is a typical Rea chord progression which falls more in line with pop than blues. This is cool because it requires a different approach to playing than simply the minor pentatonic in home position.

Having said that, Chris's approach is clear. Handling the Am chord with a double-stop at the 20th fret (highlighting the 5th and b7th), there is a shift down to the same intervals for the Dm chord at the 13th fret.

Next is a G Major chord, achieved by sliding up two frets to the home position for G Major, highlighting the 3rd and 5th.

Example 13a

The next example continues with the second part of the chord progression and adds an ending using F Major and E Major chords.

As in the previous example, Chris would find a single position for each chord and stick relatively closely to it.

The other interesting thing to note is how Chris approaches the A minor chord. Playing in an open major tuning makes minor chords a little tricky. Chris plays notes at the 20th fret which we would normally think of as C Major. C Major is the relative major of A minor. Look at a C Major chord's construction (C, E, G) and you'll see it has a lot in common with A minor (A, C, E). Add an A note under your C Major triad (A, C, E, G) and you create an Am7 chord.

Example 13b

For the next example, I've taken the entire passage and played double-stops in each position, applying vibrato. It showcases how simple, yet effective, slide playing can be. This sort of idea is great for a lead player to play during a verse.

Example 13c

Of course, Chris still plays the blues! The next lick demonstrates his approach with a line that works well over a blues in E. As with many slide players, milking vocabulary from a single string is an effective way to make a melody.

Example 13d

Finally, here's a single-note blues idea that works well on the IV to I chord movement in a 12-bar blues. In this case it's A Major going back to E Major. There's nothing wrong with the open position!

Example 13e

Chapter Fourteen – Tampa Red

Born Hudson Woodbridge in Georgia, 1903, Tampa Red would go on to be one of the early Chicago blues influences, having an impact on Robert Nighthawk, Muddy Waters, Elmore James and more.

Red moved to Florida at a young age and picked up guitar skills from his brother and local musicians. He relocated to Chicago in the 1920s, now with a unique approach to slide guitar, and was set to start his career.

His first real gig was accompanying the mother of blues, Ma Rainey. He went on to record his music with Georgia Tom as the Hokum Boys, and with Frankie Jaxon, as Tampa Red's Hokum Jug Band.

From here his career grew steadily, both as a band leader and session musician. Alongside the Chicago Five, he pioneered the "Bluebird Sound" when recording for Bluebird Records and continued putting record out right into the 1950s.

In the early '50s Red's wife passed away, and during this period he turned to drink. This would take him away from music for a while, until the blues revival of the late '50s and early '60s when he resurfaced to make a few more select recordings before hanging up his guitar for good.

Tampa Red had a long career which went through the electric revolution, so his sound changed a lot. He began on acoustic, moved onto a resonator guitar (a gold one, earning him the name "The Man With The Golden Guitar"), and eventually dabbled in electric guitar, showing that your sound is what you make it. He played in a few tunings, but open D appears to have been the most common.

Like many of these early pioneers who were lost to time, it's hard to say for sure what type of slide Tampa used, or what finger he wore it on. All we can say is that his unique approach to single-string slide improvising was a precursor to the Rock 'n' Roll that would come later.

Now, onto the licks!

First is a simple melody that Red might play in between some fingerstyle chordal work.

There's nothing complicated here, so just focus on the articulation. This is a melody and it should be treated as such. Focus on the vibrato and sliding in and out of notes. Make it sing!

Example 14a

Tampa was keen on both open D and open E tuning, but would often use a capo to change key. This example stays in open E and uses a capo at the 4th fret to raise the key to F# Major. You could just as easily play this in open D with a capo at the 2nd fret.

This line is a little faster and uses triplets, but your main focus here should be the use of the slide and the fingers of the fretting hand. Two notes need to be fretted with the index finger (indicated in the TAB with brackets).

Example 14b

Next is a great turnaround lick that subtly outlines the chord changes. Pay attention to which notes should be played with the fretting hand. They all occur in bar 3.

Example 14c

This example only uses the slide on notes indicated by a bend – everything else is played with the fretting hand fingers. I know this seems like an odd example for a slide guitar book, but being a good slide player means being able to get by with things other than single-note melodies. The chords in the turnaround are an excellent example of this skill.

Example 14d

The final example shows more of a solo guitar part. It takes a simple melody in D played on the high string, set against a thumping pedal note on the low string. In bar 3 there are some more fretted notes indicated by the brackets.

Example 14e

Chapter Fifteen – Gary Rossington

Born in Florida in 1951, Gary Rossington has the odd distinction of not playing an astonishing amount of slide guitar in his career, while having played slide on one of the most iconic rock tracks of all time.

After getting some experience playing drums, Rossington picked up the guitar aged 14 (a Sears and Roebuck Silvertone). He played in a band with friends and after several line-up changes the group eventually came to be called Lynyrd Skynyrd.

Influenced by rock and blues music of the time, and bringing a classic southern twist, Rossington admired slide players like Duane Allman (who the band used to go and see), Al Wilson, and Brian Jones, but learned to play as well as he could in standard tuning.

The group released their debut album *Lynyrd Skynyrd (Pronounced 'Lěh-'nérd 'Skin-'nérd)* in 1973. The album contained favorites such as *Gimmie Three Steps*, *Simple Man*, and the guitar epic, *Free Bird*. Aside from the legendary guitar solo, the prominence of the slide guitar part is often overlooked in this track. It was a sound Rossington would come back to time and again.

If you watch a video of the band playing *Free Bird* live, you'll see Rossington has a piece of heavy green electrical wire placed under his strings around the first fret to push the action up and make slide playing easier. This is a great trick used by many players over the years who just need to play slide for one track, so don't carry a second guitar.

The group followed their success with 1974's *Second Helping* (containing the band's best known song, *Sweet Home Alabama*), 1975's *Nuthin' Fancy*, 1976's *Gimmie Back My Bullets*, and 1977's *Street Survivors*.

At this point the band couldn't have been more successful, but tragedy hit just days after the release of *Street Survivors*. The band were involved in a plane crash that killed lead singer Ronnie Van Zant, guitarist Steve Gaines, backing singer Cassie Gaines and key members of the band's crew. The members who survived were seriously injured and Rossington broke his pelvic bone, multiple ribs, bones in his feet, both wrists, both arms and both legs.

Gary made a return with both The Rossington-Collins Band and later The Rossington Band, with each group releasing their fair share of music.

In 1987, Skynyrd would reunite with Ronnie's younger brother Johnny on vocals. The group are still active today and releaed a further 9 albums. Gary has also continued to release music as a band leader, most notably under the "Rossington" moniker, and his most recent album is 2016's *Take It On Faith*.

Gary is a long time Les Paul user, though he has been known to use a Firebird and an SG from time to time. In his current setup he has a black Les Paul with slightly higher action that he uses for slide playing. He wears a glass slide on his middle finger, and plays in standard tuning often, though he occasionally uses open E and open G tuning.

Let's take a look at some of his licks!

Of course, it would be impossible to talk about Gary's playing and not lean heavily on *Free Bird*, so the first lick is based around the slide melody from that iconic recording.

This example is an interesting one to study as the chords in the progression (G Major, D/F#, E minor, F Major, C Major, D Major) don't all come from the same key. Therefore, a single scale will not fit over the top! When soloing, our approach needs to be based around the individual chords.

In Example 15a then, the first note played on each chord is a note from the chord itself. G is the root of G Major, F# is the 3rd of D/F# and G is the b3 of E minor. Using this approach, we play an F root note when we reach the F Major chord in bar 5 that does not occur in the key of G Major and everything sounds great.

Example 15a

The second lick showcases how Rossington might play slide lead guitar lines behind a singer. The chord progression is the same, but there is a lot of space in the phrasing.

Example 15b

The next example develops this idea over the chorus progression – a repeating F Major, C Major and D Major.

The melody sticks closely to the chords, taking few risks. The excitement in the lick is produced by including almost random slides up the neck between phrases. These are never played the exact same way twice, but that's not important – what's important is exploiting the unique aspects of the slide.

Example 15c

The following lick walks the same path as the last, but now ramps up the intensity in the final two bars by playing the exact same notes as the last idea, but with a 1/16th note rhythm instead of tamer 1/8th notes.

The beauty of a lick like this is that, at speed, it can never be as cleanly executed as it would if it was fretted, but this adds to the chaotic magic of slide!

Example 15d

Our final example demonstrates something Gary might play on a track in E Major, now using just the notes of the E Major Pentatonic scale (E, F#, G#, B, C#). Something like this is much tricker to play in standard tuning, but it's beyond the realms of possibility.

Gary isn't a particularly advanced slide guitar player – he's not full of theory or chops – he just plays basic melodies, but with lots of expression. Experiment with the scale and see what happens.

Example 15e

Chapter Sixteen – Derek Trucks

Born in Jacksonville, Florida, in 1979, Derek Trucks would quickly become one of the pioneers of electric slide guitar, influencing endless guitarists to pick up a bottleneck.

Born into a musical lineage (his uncle was Butch Trucks, the long serving and original drummer in the Allman Brothers Band), Derek picked up guitar at the age of 9 when he found a beat-up acoustic guitar in a yard sale for $5.

Attracted to the sound of Duane Allman on the *Live at Fillmore East* and *Layla* records, and spurred on by his father's Elmore James records, Derek instantly understood the power of slide guitar and the way it emulated the human voice.

To describe Derek as a prodigy may be an understatment as he was out playing shows aged just 11, and even sitting in with the Allman Brothers when he was 13. Footage of these gigs is available on YouTube and it's clear that Derek could probably outplay anyone, even that early in his life.

In 1994 Trucks formed the Derek Trucks Band, which would go on to record multiple albums (and from a personal persepctive, some of my favorite albums of all time!), winning a Grammy for 2009's *Already Free*. If you have some time, 1998's *Out of the Madness* and 2002's *Joyful Noise* are must-hear albums for fans of slide guitar.

In 1999 Trucks became an official member of the Allman Brothers Band alongside Warren Haynes. He recorded just one studio album with the band, 2003's *Hittin' the Note*, along with several live releases and endless bootlegs. He spent 15 years with the band before their final show in 2014.

In 2014, Derek formed the Tedeschi Trucks Band with his wife Susan Tedeschi. To date, the group have released five studio albums, each being an absolute masterclass in expression, and one official live release. Their latest offering, 2019's *Signs*, continues to showcase what a great future Derek has in music.

Derek's slide style is extremely expressive, but technically straight ahead. There's no need for crazy advanced techniques – it's just him and a glass slide on his ring finger doing his best to imitate the human voice.

Gear wise, Derek is a long time Gibson SG user, having his own signature model. He's a straight into the amp kind of guy, riding his volume knob for maximum expression. Just like his hero, Duane Allman, he tunes almost exclusively in open E, using a set of 11s and always has an unwound 3rd string.

Let's take a look at his incredible licks.

First up is a killer lick demonstrating Derek's fluidity with the traditional tuning, coupled with his ability to play outside of the "key of the tuning" by ripping out a lick in Eb Major.

There's a hint of the familiar with some home postion based playing, though his particular sense of phrasing is incredible. It takes a considerable amount of control to play licks at this speed and still be able to slide down from notes (in this case the 11th fret on the 2nd string) so go slowly – it's essential to nail this to create the right feel.

The real twist here is the extensive use of the 6th note (C) located at the 13th fret, 2nd string. Most often players will stick to the notes two frets below the home position, but this note adds a sweet major pentatonic flavor to the lick.

Example 16a

Continuing with this Eb vibe, the following lick is played over a Gospel-type chorus that moves between Ab Major, A diminished 7 and Eb Major (or even an Eb/Bb chord if you want that sweet ascending bassline!)

Considering the jazzy undertones provided by the diminished chord, Trucks' approach to soloing in a setting like this still sticks closely to blues roots. He would likely play a mix of Eb Major Pentatonic (Eb, F, G, Bb, C) and Eb Minor Pentatonic (Eb, Gb, Ab, Bb, Db). Not all of these notes are used here, but that blend of the 6th (C) from the major and b3rd (Gb) from the minor gives this lick a sophisticated sound.

Example 16b

The next example takes inspiration from a viral clip of Derek playing with B.B. King. It keeps the blues phrasing, but is played over a chord progression more in line with Gospel and soul music.

Despite having a wonderful set of chords to play over, Derek would stick closely to the major and minor pentatonic scale from the key of the piece (in this case Ab Major). So while there is some moving around on single strings, eventually the focus is the home position at the 16th fret.

The tricky part of this lick is the timing. It's worth pointing out that Derek wouldn't be counting when playing a lick like this. Instead he's just pushing and pulling time for dramatic effect, so don't get too bogged down thinking about the rhythm. That said, if you want to take something from this lick, the tuplet of 4:3 requires you to play 4 notes in the space of 3!

Example 16c

Example 16d explores some of Derek's incredible single-note playing, similar to that heard on *Down In The Flood*.

Taking place over a C7 type vamp, Derek would combine both C Major Pentatonic (C, D, E, G, A) and the C Blues Scale (C, Eb, F, Gb, G, Bb) to create something bluesy and soulful.

The first four measures are a simple melody based around the idea of descending chromatically from G to Gb to F. That Gb is pretty spicy!

The next four bars showcase more of Derek's fluid single-note style. Ideas like this can be problematic, as getting clean notes on the top two strings with slide can be tricky without a high action. An interesting aspect of Derek's style is that he will fret with the slide from time to time when sliding between notes. It's hard to say if this is by design or something that just happens, and has become part of his sound. Either way, it's cool!

Example 16d

The final example shifts into a more up-tempo setting, this time with a 1/16th note shuffle feel. In terms of note choices, the line sticks close to the underlying G7 chord, but with a cool slide from the b5th (Db). The key to this lick is sitting on a note and repeatedly sliding down and back into it, without losing a sense of the intended pitch. Take it slow and build up accuracy of intonation.

Example 16e

Derek is undeniably one of the greatest slide players to walk the planet and it would be impossible to capture what he can do in just five licks. You would do well to go and listen to his music right now and start working out some of the cooler licks!

Chapter Seventeen – Joe Walsh

Born in Kansas, 1941, Joe Walsh has achieved a lot in his musical career. Most notably he has played a major role in the fifth bestselling band of all time, the Eagles.

Walsh was given his first guitar at the age of 10 and very quickly decided he wanted a career as a musician after he learnt *Walk Don't Run* by The Ventures.

His first recordings came with a band called The Measles, releasing two singles between 1965 and 1966. He stepped up the career ladder when he joined The James Gang in 1968. Joe remained part of the group when they became a trio and took on vocal duties. The group's debut album *Yer* was released in 1969, followed by *James Gang Rides Again* in 1970 and *Thirds* in 1971. Despite releasing classic songs like *Funk #49*, Walsh felt the group had their limitations and left in 1971.

He followed The James Gang up with Barnstorm. Despite this being a band, the group were often billed simply as "Joe Walsh". The group's self-titled debut was released in 1972 and was received quite well. It would be their 1973 follow-up record, *The Smoker You Drink, The Player You Get*, that would really show what Walsh was capable of. It was on this record that the world was introduced to *Rocky Mountain Way*. Joe also played slide guitar on Joe Vitale's debut album, *Roller Coaster Weekend* in 1974.

In 1975, Joe joined the Eagles, appearing on the groups 1976 hit record, *Hotel California*. This was followed up in 1979 with *The Long Run*. Both albums sold many millions of copies and showcased Walsh's ability to fit in with the classic Eagles sound, but bring a rockier edge when they needed it.

The group split suddenly in 1980 due to relationship tensions between Don Felder and Glen Frey and suddenly Walsh was out on his own again. Fortunately, Walsh never stopped recording his own albums, so he continued with this to great success, releasing 10 more albums between 1974 and 2012, and recording guitar parts on many collaborations, including work with Randy Newman, Ringo Starr and The Foo Fighters.

The Eagles would reunite in 1994 and, after several lawsuits, released *Long Road Out of Eden* in 2007, their first studio album in 28 years.

Joe has used almost every guitar under the sun, so it's hard to link one particular guitar to his playing, but a Les Paul in open E tuning is going to get you close enough. He uses both glass and brass slides, and wears them on his middle finger.

Now, onto his licks!

First up is a *Rocky Mountain Way* style melody in E Major.

Walsh has never been a revolutionary slide player when it comes to his approach, but he took ideas he learned from Duane Allman and applied them to his own classic tunes, as demonstrated by this simple idea that sticks strictly to the home position at the 12th fret and the notes two frets below.

Example 17a

Next is an idea in a similar vein that adds a note three frets higher than the home position on the 2nd string. Sliding into this note creates a cool variation to the basic two fret pattern which is so often played. Nothing here should present a challenge, just play with some passion!

Example 17b

The next example sticks with the E Major setting, but adds some more exciting ideas like slides up and down the neck, open strings, and some faster triplets around the 15th fret.

While there are certainly a few more notes in this lick, the notes are still all from either the E Major Pentatonic scale (E, F#, G#, B, C#) or E Minor Pentatonic scale (E, G, A, B, D).

Example 17c

Moving away from static chord vamps, the next lick moves between an A Major and E Major chord. While you could use some theory to work out the best scale for both chords (and all those things the best players do. Hendrix himself was a well-known Berklee graduate…!), you could just take the Joe approach and base your ideas around A Major at the 17th fret and E Major at the 12th fret. It's a considerably easier way to do things, and it sounds great!

Example 17d

Our final lick shows the build towards the end of a solo, using an A Major, B Major, and E Major chord progression.

Walsh would begin by playing the A Major chord around the home position at the 17th fret. As the chord changes, he would switch to something based around E at the 12th fret to create a bluesy, pentatonic "one scale fits all" vibe to end.

This mixture of giving the chords their due, but adding tension with long sections of minor pentatonic is common in all blues playing, so slide should be no different.

Example 17e

Chapter Eighteen – Muddy Waters

Born in Mississippi in 1913, the name McKinley Morganfield might leave many scratching their heads. Muddy Waters, however, the man he would become, would go on to be a household name in blues.

Waters was raised around music in his Baptist church, so singing came naturally. It wasn't until he was 17, however, that he acquired a guitar – a Stella from Sears-Roebuck that he paid just $2.50 for.

Muddy played around his local area, singing and playing guitar without any real recognition until 1941, when Alan Lomax went to Waters' house for the Library of Congress and recorded him. The result was $20 in Muddy's pocket and a record that would spur him on. As he recalled, "I carried that record up to the corner and put it on the jukebox. Just played it and played it and said, 'I can do it, I can do it.'"

In 1943, Waters moved to Chicago. Despite not yet owning an electric guitar (he would buy one the following year), Muddy quickly found a place in the scene, regularly opening for Big Bill Broonzy.

After a few years, Muddy had really begun to develop a sound and was recording for a few labels, but success would come when the guitarist partnered with Aristocrat Records, who would go on to be known as Chess Records. Singles like *I Can't Be Satisfied, I Feel Like Going Home, Rollin' Stone, Hoochie Coochie Man* and *I'm Ready* launched Muddy into commercial success, making him a must-see act on the club scene.

In the late 50s, Waters travelled to Europe and changed everything when he played loud electric blues and slide guitar to audiences who were expecting traditional acoustic blues material. While this was offputting to many (music has always had that sub-section which rejects change), many also found this new Chicago blues sound exciting and changed their own musical direction.

As his career continued, so did his success. Between 1972 and 1980, he won six Grammy awards for Best Ethnic or Traditional Folk Recording. Three albums during this period, beginning with 1977's *Hard Again*, were produced by Johnny Winter!

Waters died of heart failure in his sleep in 1983, but his influence would go on forever, both as a forefather of the blues music that followed and as a cultural icon.

Muddy played many guitars over the course of his career, but was best known for playing a Telecaster. He would tune this to open G most often, and wore a brass slide on his pinky finger.

Let's look at some of his best known licks!

First up us a riff idea based on the classic hit, *I Can't Be Satisfied*.

The idea with this line is to alternate between high notes for the melody and open position notes to create a rhythm guitar vibe.

Pay close attention to the audio recording on this one as Waters' style is pretty reserved compared to many others in this book. There's a precision to his playing with a subtle controlled vibrato.

Example 18a

When watching any live footage of Muddy, you'll quickly notice just how much he can milk out of a single string, as shown the following example illustrates.

The other thing of note here is just how slow some blues tracks are. This one clocks in at 50bpm, which leaves you a ton of space to play with, but for this style, less is definitely more.

In open G tuning, the highest string isn't tuned to the root of the G chord, instead it's the 5th (D). The root note is found at the 5th fret, so this will always sound like home.

Example 18b

Another noteworthy aspect of Muddy Waters' playing is his use of the slide in conjunction with fretted notes. The following outlines the last four bars of a 12-bar blues in G Major and features a classic Waters turnaround lick. Fretted notes played with the finger descend chromatically, played against an open string. Aside from this one measure, the rest is executed with the slide as normal.

While I've notated this as only having an open 3rd string, it will sound just as good if you leave the 2nd string open too. Experiment and have fun!

Example 18c

Here's another take on the same turnaround lick. This time it's been dressed up with a few more single note ideas.

One fascinating aspect of Waters' playing on a lick like this (not to mention all the old blues guys) is just how out of tune some of the slides can be. When you're reading a book on technique, you might find this hard to deal with, but those old blues slide players weren't concerned with our nice neat 12-tone system. It was all about expression, so when you're sliding to a note (like the 3rd fret in this lick), you're really playing somewhere *between* the 3rd and 4th frets.

Example 18d

The final example mixes thing up a little with a turnaround on a blues in D. (It's worth noting that the track that inspired this lick was played with a capo, making the key Bb. Waters often played with a capo).

This idea sticks largely to a single string and shifts between pitches in a bluesy manner. The only part to take note of here is that the final measure is fretted with the fingers, not played with the slide!

Example 18e

Chapter Nineteen – Bukka White

Born in Mississippi, 1906, Bukka White would forge a legacy as one of the iconic Delta blues guitarists of the golden era.

Like many musicians of this era, the details surrounding White's early life are speculative. In fact, his date of birth and location are often debated – and not by a day or two, but by 8 years! Some have reported that he got his first guitar aged 9. He had music lessons, but his grandmother made it very clear that she didn't want anyone playing "that Devil music" so he kept his passion hidden.

Realising that playing guitar brought him attention from the opposite sex, a 14-year old White began to take music a lot more seriously, and things gathered momentum when he met Charley Patton.

In the '30s and '40s White had flirtations with success, but this was marred by circumstances and he was imprisoned for shooting a man. Despite spending three years locked away, he continued to further his career. Everyone he met, from inmates to guards, were drawn to his personality and music.

After serving his sentence he recorded his most loved sessions for Lester Melrose. During this time he recorded *Parchman Farm Blues, Good Gin Blues, Bukk's Jitterbug Swing, Aberdeen, Mississippi Blues, Fixin' to Die Blues*, and more. All would go on to be considered classics of the Delta blues genre.

Unfortunately, the war took White away from music and, like several artists in this book, he just disappeared for a long time. During the '60s he was unearthed when John Fahey and Ed Denson posted a letter addressed to "Bukka White (Old Blues Singer), c/o General Delivery, Aberdeen Mississippi" and somehow it managed to filter through to him via a family member.

This '60s period saw a huge resurgence for White as he donned his suit and went out to play regularly. He thrived on the attention and recorded three albums, but it wasn't until he took the time to go back and listen to the original Melrose recordings and relearn how "classic White" played that he really became the man his audience had imagined.

White died of cancer in 1977 in Memphis.

Despite yearning to give electric guitar a try in later life, Bukka never strayed far from his National resonator guitar, which he tuned to many chords, but most notably open D minor (D, A, D, F, A, D), sometimes called cross note tuning. He played with a metal slide on his pinky finger. As for his music, he simply played what he lived.

Let's check out some of his ideas.

First is a classic Delta slide style riff, alternating the 6th and 4th strings with the thumb and playing a melody on top with the slide.

Use the slide for the notes on the high string. You'll probably find fretting the note on the 2nd string easiest.

Example 19a

The second lick takes the same thumping rhythm concept, but now with a melody using the D Minor Pentatonic scale (D, F, G, A, C).

Playing in a minor key makes a lot of sense given Bukka's tuning, but in this case you're not actually playing the F string, so this lick will work fine in open D *or* D minor.

Example 19b

The next example employs the same basic idea as the last two examples, but adds more notes on the upbeats between the notes played with the thumb.

While there are many ways to execute this idea, Bukka would have just used his thumb for the notes in the bass and index finger for the melody notes. Other than that, keep the note with the slide ringing throughout.

Example 19c

Next we'll attempt to get wild, the same way Bukka would when he played solo slide parts. There is still a separation between chord and melody parts, but this example is strummed quite wildly! Bukka would use a thumbpick here to get the upstrokes on beat 3. The thumb is going: down, down, down up, down... over and over, like a riff, but the slide melody is added over the top.

Example 19d

Our final example showcases how Bukka uses the slide to slide between notes in a melody. Like the previous examples, keep the thumb going while adding the melody on top. Note that the 2nd fret on the 2nd string is fretted with a finger rather than the slide.

Example 19e

Bukka White had one of the wildest, unrefined sounds of anyone in this book, and learning to play like him will never come from words on a page. You need to go and listen to his music and do everything you can to copy the attitude of his playing.

Good luck!

Chapter Twenty – Johnny Winter

Born in Texas in 1944, Johnny Winter was raised in a musical family, with a father who played saxophone and guitar at various public events. This clearly appealed to Johnny and his brother, as by the age of 10, they were performing on children's shows with Johnny playing ukulele.

After some minor success in his late teens, in 1968 Johnny decided to focus his efforts on blues-rock. After releasing *The Progressive Blues Experiment* locally, things changed when Rolling Stone Magazine wrote a glowing review of Johnny and his playing, calling him the next big thing. This was enough to attract serious management and, before he knew it, labels were fighting over him. In the end, CBS won out with a record breaking $600k advance – the most the label had ever shelled out on a new solo artist.

Winter's first two albums on Colombia (1969's *Johnny Winter* and *Second Winter*) were big successes, and even landed him a spot at Woodstock.

Despite being dogged by heroin addiction, the '70's were still a successful period for Johnny, both with his new backing band, and through producing three Grammy award winning albums for one of his guitar idols, Muddy Waters.

From here he continued to record album after album for various labels, until he was found dead in his hotel room in Switzerland in 2014. Until this point, Johnny's only success at the Grammys was with Muddy Waters, but 2014's *Step Back* was posthumously awarded Best Blues Album.

Winter was an influence to many, and did much to help the careers of the people he looked up to. This spirit of positivity is still heard in his music by fans today.

Johnny was a long-time fan of the Gibson Firebird, with his main guitar being a '63 V model. The V model differed from previous offerings as they featured the mini-humbucker, something Johnny was particularly fond of. "It feels like a Gibson, but it sounds closer to a Fender than most other Gibsons," he said. "I was never a big fan of humbucking pickups, but the mini-humbuckers on the Firebird have more bite and treble."

He played with a thumbpick and his fingers, and used the same piece of metal pipe as a slide, worn on his pinky finger, for his entire career. Now that's impressive!

Let's look at some of his legendary licks.

This first idea is inspired by Johnny's classic *Highway 61 Revisited*. It showcases some slick open position ideas in open D tuning.

There's nothing revolutionary here, just a good combination of D major and minor pentatonics, all executed with some attitude.

Example 20a

Example 20b continues the idea, but jumps from higher up the neck to the same basic riff seen before.

Slide into the 2nd and 3rd strings at the 15th fret, and let them ring out with some vibrato to add excitement. Then play the open position lick before sliding back up the neck to the 12th fret home position.

Example 20b

The next example shows how much mileage Johnny can get out of one idea, this time offsetting the open position idea by a few beats (playing it early) and extending it out at the end.

After the fast-paced lead part, shift up to the 7th fret for the V chord (A), then back to the 12th fret home position for the I chord (D).

Example 20c

When it comes to soloing, Johnny was no stranger to playing around the home position of whatever key he was in, as demonstrated in the following example.

The twist here is offsetting the higher notes against open strings. This technique created huge intervallic leaps in his licks and elevated Winter above average position-based slide players. They're also quite tricky to execute at speed. I recommend picking the first note with the middle finger, then the next with the index, followed by the thumb on the 2nd string. Take your time with the mechanics of the lick and build up speed over time.

Example 20d

The final example takes the idea of Example 20b but adds high string into the ringing notes for some real high energy blues rock.

After two bars of playing around the 12th fret area, you're back to the open position for an idea similar to each example in this chapter. The point here is that it's possible to milk endless musical ideas out of just a few basic patterns. The masters of this style often had limited vocabulary, but their mastery lay in how they used that vocabulary to express themselves – so get to work!

Example 20e

Perfect Your Slide Guitar Technique with Levi Clay

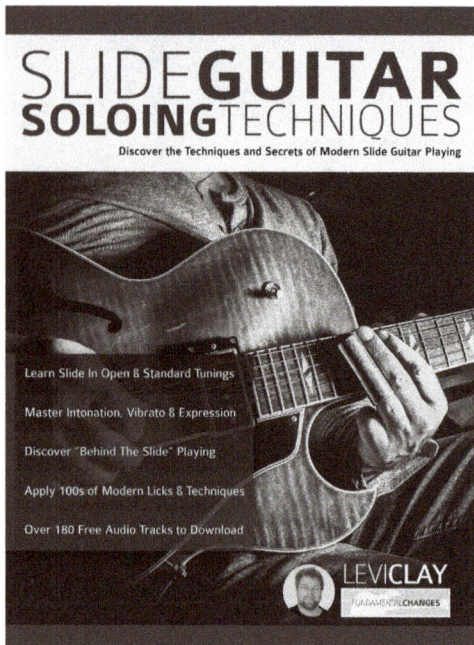

Slide guitar is currently enjoying a huge renaissance thanks to contemporary players like **Derek Trucks, Joey Landreth, Brett Garsed, AJ Ghent** and **Jack White** – great innovators who are carrying the flame for the next generation.

Learning how to play slide guitar is one of the few techniques can change your whole approach to the guitar, so much so that it becomes a whole new instrument. In this book, you will master the art and technique of modern electric slide guitar playing.

What You'll Learn:

- Essential open tunings for slide, & scale shapes for innovative soloing
- Advanced guitar techniques such as playing behind the slide, false harmonics & legato
- Slide guitar licks in style of **Duane Allman, Ry Cooder** and **Johnny Winter**

- Modern techniques from **Derek Trucks, Dan Auerbach, Joey Landreth** and **Brett Garsed**
- The rarely taught skill of playing slide guitar in standard tuning!

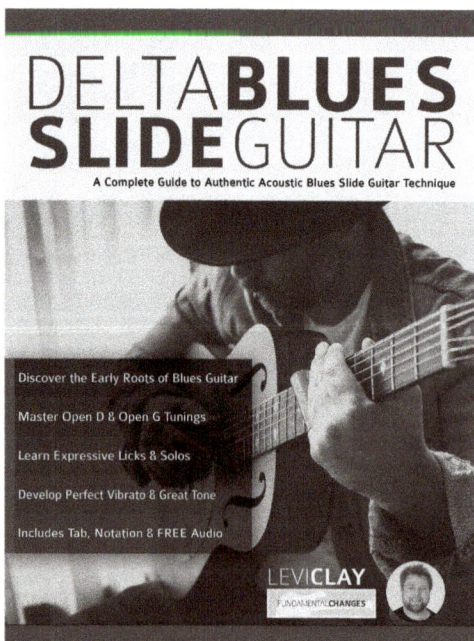

Delta Blues Slide Guitar is a complete guide to the techniques and music of "bottleneck" acoustic blues – a genre that can be traced back over 100 years to the Mississippi Delta. It's where blues guitar was first heard over 60 years before Led Zeppelin, Eric Clapton and others brought it to the masses.

This ground-breaking slide guitar book teaches the art of flawless Delta slide guitar technique through hundreds of exercises and three full-length songs that help you to master each skill in a musical, confident way.

You'll learn guitar licks in the style of the Delta Blues slide pioneers, such as **Robert Johnson, Son House, Bukka White** and **Tampa Red**, and learn complete songs with performance notes and guidance.

You'll also receive tips and insights on choosing the right slide, finding the best left-hand technique for you, and suggestions for recommended listening.

www.ingramcontent.com/pod-product-compliance
Lightning Source LLC
Chambersburg PA
CBHW081432090426
42740CB00017B/3272